POOR BABY
A Child of the 60's Looks Back on Abortion

by
Heather King

Copyright © Heather King, 2012

COVER PHOTO:

May, 1958, me, age 5, on the steps of the Rhode Island farmhouse where my mother was raised.

FOR CHRISTINE LOWE

Etymology
Latin

From *aborior* ("pass away; miscarry"), from *ab* ("of, by, from") + *orior*.
(*Classical*) IPA: /ˈo.ri.or/

Verb

Present active orior, *present infinitive* orīrī, *perfect active* ortus sum. (deponent)

1. I rise, get up.

2. I appear, become visible.

3. I am born, come to exist, originate.

POOR BABY

I came of age during the '60's and '70's. I'm a former waitress, an ex-lawyer, a sober drunk, and a self-supporting writer. I've been financially independent all my life. But I've never much been able to reduce the mystical to the political. I've never been much moved to call myself a feminist. The feminists had said that sleeping around would be empowering. The feminists had maintained that "choosing" would make me free. The feminists had asserted that there'd be no repercussions. The feminists had been wrong.

The feminists had been wrong, but I'd always known they were wrong. Every guy I'd ever slept with, for example, no matter how inappropriate or unavailable, I'd pretty much instantly wanted to be my boyfriend, if not marry. What was the *matter* with me? I'd wondered for a long time. Why did I have to be such a *sap*? Later, I'd realized you *should* have feelings for the person with whom you have sex. Later—too late—I'd realize you *should* have feelings for the kid, or in my case kids, you'd conceived.

Through getting sober, getting married, moving from Boston to L.A., a (mercifully brief) legal career, quitting my job to become a writer, a divorce, my first book, my second book, I had flourished. I had survived. My life had meaning and point. Los Angeles—so maddening, so glorious—was a fount of the paradoxes on which my creative imagination thrived. I rented a beautiful apartment in a bad part of town. I took long, solitary walks through my over-crowded neighborhood and cooked elaborate dinners for friends. I trudged to Mass, and I drove to the women's jail in Watts and talked to the inmates about addiction. I complained about the cacophony of ice cream trucks, car alarms, leaf blowers, and hordes of screaming children, and I also knew that the riotous mass of humanity against which I daily rubbed up provided the tension necessary to fuel and maintain my inner life. I wrote—above all, I wrote—and while I waited with much of the rest of the city for a crumb of news from my agent, I availed myself of the public library, the strip-mall pho joints, the thrift stores with their five-buck Levis and leather jackets, the light that streamed down from the mountains like a benediction.

I was absorbed, energized, engaged. I was not depressed. I did not need or want medication. But beneath the surface ran a searing, aching loneliness; a subliminal sense of sorrow so acute I once looked up the word "keen" in the dictionary in order to confirm that "a prolonged wail for a deceased person" was precisely the cry silently emanating from one corner of my heart. I had done what I could to ease the pain. I had told of my past, if the part in question only glancingly, to spiritual directors and friends. A Catholic convert, I had been to Confession. What was done was done—and yet, one part of my face I could never show; one part of my psyche was so shrouded in darkness that even I, who make a life's work of pondering, analyzing, contemplating, could not fully access it.

That I instinctively avoided children, tensed up when passing toy stores and playgrounds, and blanched at the phrase "baby shower" I had come to accept as simply part of my hard-wiring. Finally, however, I made the connection that I couldn't, or wouldn't, make before. Early in 2010, I realized that the three abortions I'd had over two decades earlier were not fading increasingly into the background, as I'd kept expecting, but claiming ever more of my attention.

We're very concerned these days that everyone is given a "voice," but one person nobody wants to hear from is the woman who's had an abortion. One side says: *What I do in bed is my business*; the other side says: *You made your bed; now lie in it.* The left doesn't want to hear from the woman who's had an abortion because to feel remorse, shame, or doubt is to betray "the cause." The right doesn't want to hear from the woman who's had an abortion because you're going to burn in hell so why should *you* matter? The priest doesn't want to hear, particularly, from the woman who's had an abortion because the issue is way too complex, multi-layered, and potentially time-consuming; women, as we all know, get weird around sex, men, and children; the priest, being human, probably hasn't worked out all those things within himself; and besides, *you've been forgiven,* so let's

forego opening *that* can of worms and move on.

Even women, who will talk about *anything,* don't talk

about abortion. Women, who within five minutes of being

introduced will know each other's career and relationship

status, family situation, taste in clothing, food, movies, books,

and men, don't talk about abortion. I think this is because

women, of all people, know that abortion is a failure of love.

Women know that if the guy with whom you were sleeping

loved you enough, chances are you would have had his baby

in a heartbeat. Women know that no matter how superficially

relieved you may have felt immediately afterwards; no matter

how financially, emotionally, and logistically impossible having

a kid just then would have been; no matter how much

sympathy they may (or may not) have for you and your

situation, you've still gone against your deepest soul: against

everything in you that is most precious, most worthy, most

inviolate.

The fact that I had so egregiously gone against my own

deepest soul lay squarely, forever, with me. I did not blame the women's movement. I did not blame the men with whom I had slept. But I did begin to see that, as contemplative writer Ron Rolheiser has observed: "In a culture which is sexually irresponsible the inevitable losers are women. They end up suffering the most."

This is not a political idea; it's a human idea: which is to say an idea leading away from victim-hood and toward maturity. Maturity means consenting to develop a conscience. Maturity means acknowledging that there are always consequences; there are always repercussions. Maturity compelled me to admit that sexual responsibility had hardly been *my* forte: the fathers of the first two children I'd aborted had both been married. And the father of the third child I aborted I'd been engaged to marry myself.

I once did a radio interview in which the conversation turned to abortion. Afterward, the host said, "Forgive me, but since you went the easy route by not having children, people might think it's hypocritical for you to speak on abortion. You may not quite have the *right* to a voice." That's one way of looking at it. Another would be that women who have had abortions are the *most* qualified to speak. If not me—and women like me—who, then? The woman who didn't have an abortion and regrets it? Bring her on. Let's see the woman who is dying to point to her kid and tell the world: *This is the biggest mistake of my life. I'd give her away now if I could. The world would be a richer, more joyful, more peaceful place had I destroyed my daughter in the womb.*

Bring that woman on if you can find her. Bring all such women on. You're going to find very, very few, if any, because we all know that *once you have the kid, you will love him or her. And then where will you be*? We all know what happens when you love someone. You turn into a fool! You make crazy sacrifices! You do without all kinds of things that in your right mind you wouldn't dream of doing without! "

There is only one thing I dread," said Dostoevsky: "not to be worthy of my sufferings."

Maybe I don't have a right to talk about abortion in the sense that I was not at the time worthy of my suffering. But surely we always have a right to say: *I was not worthy of my suffering, and I wish I had been.*

When we talk about abortion we are really talking about the function and meaning of suffering, which is why everybody tends to get so hot under the collar when the subject is raised. The most radical, most incendiary, most taboo subject is not sex or money or politics or even death, but suffering. Nothing will get you killed faster than suggesting that the meaning of life is to be found in our relationship to suffering. Nothing challenges the existing order more; nothing so strongly threatens our bodily, mental, emotional and spiritual integrity; nothing makes us so proprietary about our identity, our organizing principles.

Everyone likes to think, *Of course I'm compassionate. Of course my life is geared toward alleviating suffering.* But most of the time our lives are only geared in that direction if we're going to gain by our actions; if we're serving ourselves. When we see the frightful, endless suffering of the world we don't tend to think, for example, *Let me forego this act that would bring me instant gratification but that is not toward the greater good.* We don't tend to think, *Let me take the beam out of my own eye before I try to take the beam out of my neighbor's eye.* We don't tend to ask ourselves, *How honest am I, how vulnerable, how selfish*? We tend to think instead, *I'd <u>like</u> to be less selfish, but the world isn't set up that way.* We tend to think, *You go first. You change, and then maybe I'll change. You be vulnerable, and then I'll be vulnerable. You stop waging war, then I'll stop waging war. But first—let's have sex!*

I began to realize that there had to be legions of women—and possibly men—walking around bearing this same harrowing, isolating burden. I began, tentatively, to broach the subject to people I knew. Female friends of decades-long standing confided that they, too, had had an abortion (or more than one); they, too, had kept their feelings and thoughts under wraps. One friend with three grown children was still haunted by the abortion she'd had as a teenager. Another, though wanting the child, had had an abortion at the insistence of her partner, only to be promptly dumped, then watch the guy go off, find a hotter, younger babe, proceed to father a whole family, and by all accounts live happily ever after. Maybe the most wrenching conversation was with a man, a film critic and former junkie. He said his wife had had multiple abortions before they were married. He said she'd been to a slew of therapists since, but had never made her peace. He said he himself had never quite recovered from the unilateral decision of a long-ago ex-girlfriend to abort the child they'd conceived. "He'd be thirty now, my son," he said. *How strange*, I kept thinking afterward. *He "knew" the child was male.*

Not every woman to whom I talked had similar feelings. A few said, in so many words, "I'm glad I didn't have a kid. I would have been a horrible mother."

But does any woman who gets an abortion think she'd be a great mother? That I thought I would have been a bad mother went without saying. That I assumed I would have been a horrible mother—that I was incompetent, that I had no capacity for love, that the guy would bail—was the whole problem: a mindset emblematic of a life based on way too much fear and not nearly enough faith; on way too much craving for anesthesia and not nearly enough hunger for the truth.

Speaking of the truth, I couldn't play both ends from the middle. I couldn't think the people who believed, say, that the world was created in seven days, were pitiful primitives and also, after looking at photos of fetal development, refuse to concede that life begins at conception. I might not have believed that life was worthy of being protected but integrity demanded I acknowledge that it was life. I might not have believed it wrong to destroy that life but integrity demanded that I at least acknowledge I had destroyed it. In fact, however, I *did* believe that life was worthy of being protected. I *did* think destroying that life was wrong. I'd known it was wrong before I ever looked at any photo.

One truth transcends all politics, science, commerce, technology, and culture; all peer pressure, ridicule, and scorn; all time, all space, all history. That is the truth of the human heart. In the human heart, things are not hip, arch, sophisticated, cynical, clever, effective, self-righteous, self-justifying, or convenient. They're simple and childlike. They're either right, which is to say toward love; or they're wrong, which is to say away from it. You don't have to be a theologian to believe that human beings have souls. You don't have to be a metaphysician to feel an instinctive urge to protect life, especially life that is weaker than you. A kid cries at the death of a kitten. A kid will protect a bird's egg.

I'm not talking about sentimentality, which has been defined as giving to a thing more tenderness than God gives to it. Sentimentality is why so much of the discussion about abortion rings false. We don't have any other imagery, so we use the image of babies. Then we pretend that babies, for all the joy they (apparently) bring, aren't in another way a giant pain in the rear. We pretend a baby doesn't blow the life of the parents, especially the mother, apart. We pretend babies don't grow into first children, then teenagers, then adults who suffer unbelievably and inflict suffering on others—because suffering is what life, in large part, consists. Not every child is going to be born into an ideal situation. Some people are going to better parents—way better—than others. Some children are going to be more rejoiced over than others. That's the way the world is: messy, awkward, unpredictable, inconsistent and inconvenient. That's reality.

Reality is also the only place where we can hope to find authentic transcendence, mystery, humor, connection, and joy—which is exactly why sentimentality is so dangerous. The right tends to be sentimental toward babies, and to have no tenderness at all toward the single mothers and the often disenfranchised, troubled, hungry, lonely, uninsured, uneducated children they struggle to raise alone after choosing to bring their pregnancies to term. The left purports to be more tender than God by trying to head all such suffering off at the pass. *We will save the unwanted child from suffering by destroying it*, the thinking goes. *We will save the mother from suffering by helping her to take the shortcut. We will save the father*—but then we don't have to save the father. The father, as always, can walk away any time he likes. We've never had to save the father. That's one reason both the left and the right miss the mark; why reducing abortion to a political issue still leaves the woman holding the bag.

That's also why my blood runs cold whenever I see a guy, purporting to be on the side of women, aggressively supporting abortion. I recently learned that David Foster

Wallace, God rest his soul, apparently once made a comment to the effect that his goal as a writer was to teach his readers that they were smarter than they thought they were. *I beg your pardon*, I wanted to retort, *but I do not need you to teach me how smart I am*. That's how I feel toward men who support abortion. Don't do me any favors. Please. I don't need you to promote my "rights." I don't need you to condescend, patronize, and purport to have the faintest, slightest idea of what it is to be a woman expecting a child, especially when you stand to get more no-strings-attached sex from the deal than ever. I love men, but could anyone possibly stand to "gain" more from abortion—in the sense of being let off the hook when they shouldn't be—than they do?

Beneath abortion lies the split between men and women depicted in the story of the Garden of Eden; the rift decreeing that henceforward, we would all be baffled, bewildered, longing to connect; all aching for each other and afraid of each other. But how, as women, can we possibly expect to heal the split by overprotecting men; by bearing in our bodies, souls, and nervous systems a burden that should be theirs to share; by remaining silent; by pretending that sustaining this almost mortal wound doesn't hurt and doesn't matter; by confusing the private with the secret and furtive?

If abortion is so wonderful, why are we so reluctant to expose it to the light? Why, at the clinic, do they use the word "procedure?" Why, when gazing into the bassinet of our friend's newborn baby do we not tend to exclaim: "Adorable! I aborted mine!" Everyone's on board for the sex, but no-one likes to think of what transpires afterward for the woman who aborts. No long, hot kisses then. No delighted tandem gaze at the ultrasound: *Oh honey, look at his tiny feet!* Afterward does not bear looking at, thinking about, or in any particular remembering. That's why for so long I had not wanted to know. My mind would go so far and no further.

The fact is you get crucified if you have the kid; you get crucified if you don't. Fire or fire. The redemptive suffering of taking responsibility for your actions; the neurotic (because avoidable) suffering of failing to. I just don't see any way around this. I don't think there is a way around it: hence, I am the Way, the Truth, and the Life. The cross—which I mention partly because as I said, I'm a Catholic (I converted, for the record, after my abortions) and partly because we claim to be a Christian nation—is a picture of the human psyche. Jacques Fesch was a Parisian who shot a cop, was sentenced to death, and had a conversion experience in prison. "It's only a short time since I really understood what the cross is," he wrote before going to the guillotine in 1957. "It is simultaneously miraculous and horrifying. Miraculous, because it gives us life, horrifying because if we do not bring about our own crucifixion, we have no access to life."

That's something you tend not to hear from either the "pro-lifers" or the "pro-choicers"—nor nearly enough, for that matter, in church. I once heard a truly dreadful homily from a priest who told of a baby who'd been "saved" from abortion. Twenty years later, the "baby" was a strapping blond quarterback with a 4.0 at Notre Dame. No-one would want to take that away from the guy, but why not choose as your pro-life poster child a 20-year-old with Down syndrome, or a flaming drag queen, or an abscessed meth freak? Why not acknowledge that a good percentage of the babies who are "saved" are going to become broken-down homeless people, illegal immigrants, and vicious criminals?

That of course is no reason to promote abortion; in fact, that's the very reason abortion is wrong. Let's remember who we're dealing with here, folks: the unfathomable human race. We're all bothersome. We're all, in our ways, broken. Which somehow makes it all the more imperative that we not lose a single member. We're responsible for each other. We live and die by each other. We need all the help we can get.

That we're saving saints is one false picture of abortion. Another is that the typical abortion-seeker is a nine-year-old victim of rape by her fat, drunken stepfather. In fact, according to the statistics I dug up, less than 1% of abortions are sought in response to rape or incest (not that even one case of rape or incest is good news). The three major reasons, more or less, are in fact "negative impact on the mother's life," "financial instability," and "relationship problems/unwillingness to be a single mother." Scrolling through several such lists, I could feel all over again the cold sweat, the terror, the thoughts circling round and round: *Where am I gonna get the money to raise a kid?... Not steady enough on my feet...*

Don't even bother telling him...

Where is the guy? Where is ever the guy?...

Maybe that long-ago radio interviewer had been right in saying I'd taken the easy way, but abortion had also proven to be the lonely way. Loneliness was the abiding theme of my life, and though childhood was another psychic neighborhood I liked to avoid, much less linger in, the current pain was so intense I was almost being forced to re-visit childhood now. One of eight kids (the oldest of my parents' six), I'd been raised in a family affected by generations of alcoholism in which I had learned at a very young age that displaying feelings, making a mistake, or having needs was dangerous. Love, I believed, was a commodity in scant supply; to be striven for, hard-earned, and hoarded. From the start, I'd been over-achieving and hyper-responsible: a straight-A student who'd won the spelling bee and the talent contest and the American Legion award and graduated valedictorian of my eighth-grade class and had still felt like a fraud, a failure, and a fluke.

Also from an early age I'd had a secret, hidden life: the world of books; the call of the introspective, sensitive heart to be a writer. My parents—loving, decent, self-sacrificing—were nonetheless ill-equipped to encourage such a call, and so I refrained from ever voicing it. Instead, I graduated from high school and embarked upon what would turn out to be twenty years of hard drinking, one-night stands, the flagrant desolation of the female barfly. In college, I majored in Social Service rather than creative writing, because I wanted to be good and I thought that meant "helping" people. I went on to earn a law degree because I wanted to be loved and I thought pursuing a goal of my own would be selfish and pushy.

I got sober in 1987, then embarked upon a fourteen-year marriage through which my husband and I had both faithfully soldiered but that had begun with—had centered upon—a death, and that almost inevitably had not lasted. I stayed—seeking and striving and pondering nonetheless; becoming a writer, becoming a Catholic—because I believed marriage was a sacrament and I abhorred breaking a vow. The divorce was preceded by the slow, cruel death of my father, and followed by a bout with breast cancer. And after I'd

worked so hard to not despair, to stay standing, to become

awake and joyful and alive and spiritually mature, on the eve

of the divorce I'd fallen hopelessly in love—perhaps

subconsciously been compelled to fall in love—with someone

who didn't, or couldn't, love me back. Everything I had never

been able to offer a man before—emotional generosity, a

semblance of purity, my passion for cooking, music, writing,

books—I had offered, and my offering had been rejected. I

had yearned to create something that was bigger than either

of us and my desires had come to a stillbirth. I'd turned 50 by

that time, and that I would die a dry well, having failed at the

one thing that mattered on earth, was a grief so extreme that

some days I could hardly breathe.

Here's the real secret sorrow of abortion: the desire to

get rid of the unborn is also a desire to get rid of the women

who get pregnant with them: people who don't fit in, people

who don't get it, poor people, unlucky people, people who

think if you sleep with the guy he'll love you, people who think

sex is the only thing they have to offer, people who hunger

and thirst for connection, people who have difficulty believing that there will be enough: money, support, love.

People who believe there will be enough don't tend to get dolled up on a Saturday night (as I had during "the dark years)," make their way down to the local cesspool bar, and sit there hoping against the hope that at closing time the racist, misogynist bartender will deign to come home with them. People who believe there will be enough don't tend to keep a cigarette butt and a plastic comb in a little box, like a reliquary, to be brought out every so often and tenderly wept over: mementoes of The One upon whom for me, the sun rose and set, and to whom I was just another one-night stand. People who believe there will be enough trust, love, and support don't abort the child they conceive with their fiancé: they're yearning to bring the kid to term; they want that kid more than anything on earth, no matter how much of a stretch.

Here's another truth: when you do something that goes against your deepest soul, you feel guilty. I *should* have felt guilty. Not the sickly, self-obsessed guilt that worries about being punished, or thinks sex is wrong, but the guilt that came from knowing I'd had an opportunity to walk toward the light

and I'd blown it. I'd had an opportunity to help repair the

hemorrhaging heart of mankind and I'd torn it further asunder.

As the Swiss mystic and philosopher Father Maurice

Zundel observed:

"We are not interchangeable. We cannot put ourselves
in someone else's place. Each one of us is unique,
irreplaceable, and if human love means anything, it is because
it offers the possibility of showing this unique face that we are
to someone else. Each soul is unique. If it were not so, it
would be terrible. The soul is not some kind of mill open to
anyone, but it is a secret, a unique mystery which will never be
seen again, indispensable to the world order and the
obliteration of which would disturb the order of the universe."

I had disturbed the order of the universe, and I believed

that to disturb the order of the universe has eternal

consequences. Faith to me was an encounter with the eternal:

an ongoing event in which the tiniest thought, word, deed

"registered." At the same time, faith was also a minute-by-

minute walk with Christ in the simplest, most mundane

aspects of my daily life: my work, my relationships, my

brokenness, my weakness, my pride. My central paradigm

was forever the parable of the Prodigal Daughter/Son: that I

had squandered my inheritance in the mire and been

welcomed back to the table, no questions asked; that I had been shown such unmerited, infinite mercy had awakened in me a corresponding thirst for the infinite, as well as the knowledge that God was closer to me than my own heart.

To believe that our actions have eternal consequences gives rise to feelings not easily resolved by psychotherapy, or yoga, or eating organic. I'd addressed my own feelings over the years by, among other things, prayer, the Sacraments, and massive amounts of inner work—examinations of conscience, inventories of resentments and fears, writing and sharing with another my sexual and emotional history.

And though I'd come a long, long way—toward maturity, toward healing—mentally and psychically I still often seemed engaged in a fight-to-the-death, losing, battle. I could be harsh and judgmental, both with others and myself. I often woke from sleep at war with an unseen adversary: subconsciously intent on establishing that I was "right," on defending myself, on proving my innocence.

But I could not defend myself. No adequate excuse existed. By any worldly notion of justice I was doomed: a mother who had destroyed, killed if I had to use the word, my own children.

Without grace, the door would remain forever locked. Without more mercy (and wasn't my account overdrawn already?), there was no escape. I couldn't hope to move forward unless I started by asking: *Could I have ever been that misguided, that blind, that astray?* I couldn't hope to progress until I was willing to expose the accumulated pain of a lifetime to the light and ask for help.

So twenty-plus years after the fact, I sought help. I hadn't even been sure help existed, but "post-abortion counseling," as it's known—from secular to Jewish, Christian, New Age, Buddhist and beyond—turned out to be a going concern. Folks—especially, I am bound to say, Catholics—can be creepy around the issue so I drew near with caution. But as Flannery O'Connor observed, the central Christian mystery is that life, "for all its horror, has been found by God to be worth dying for." That mystery was the ground of my existence. Others would find an alternate way more helpful, for my part I could not imagine approaching an issue that impinged so deeply upon my capacity for love, my sexuality, my body, except through Christ—which is to say, through his Church.

After several wrong turns, I happened upon Project Rachel, a nation-wide organization with a local chapter operating under the Archdiocese of L.A. I don't remember to whom I spoke—possibly more than one person—but I remember the words because I clung to them as a drowning person clings to a raft. "Yes, we'll be glad to help," I heard. I heard, "Don't worry about paying." "You have carried this for a long time." "You are not alone.""

Thus it came to be that one afternoon a couple of weeks later, I drove to the suburb of Rosemead, found my way to the Pregnancy Help Center—a New England-style, one-story Cape Cod-type house in the middle of a strip mall— and was ushered by a pleasant receptionist into a room whose dominant feature was an anatomically correct plastic model of a womb with a fetus in it.

Here, I met with a woman named Christine, who was married with grown children and had been working with people like me for thirty-two years.

"Why don't you tell me your story," she said. "Just tell your story, in your own words." And so I told my story, and she listened. Can we ever calculate the value of a single human being who will listen? I tend to rush when I speak, afraid people will lose interest, or simply get up and leave, but Christine appeared to have all the time in the world. It was not a pretty story. The unvarnished story of abortion is not a story in which it is ever possible to appear to good advantage. I wrung my hands, and repeatedly choked up with tears, and kept my eyes on the carpet until the very end, at which point I looked up, met Christine's eyes, and found they held but a single emotion: compassion.

"Of all the people in the universe," she pointed out when I finished, "you're the one to whom your children are most connected."

That notion alone floored me. I'd thought maybe calling the beings I'd conceived "children" was other-worldly and weird. And if they were children, I'd considered myself the *last* person on earth worthy to have a relationship with them. "Really? ...I can...I'm allowed to actually think of them as my children?" I asked, and Christine assured me that I could.

Already, halfway through this first session, already I could feel

a whole new realm opening up. Just sitting across from

Christine, I saw that deep down, I'd never felt myself fully

forgiven; couldn't believe I'd been forgiven. The very idea

made me want to burst into tears, get mad, go off by myself

and brood. I'd never truly acknowledged the fullness of what

I'd done, never turned to Jesus with my whole heart and said *I*

see it, I feel it, I'm so, so sorry: Lord Jesus Christ, have mercy

on me, a sinner. I'd been afraid that what I'd done was too big

for me to go to God with it. I'd thought even Christ would turn

away his face. But really I had turned my face, or a part of it,

away from him. The most tender, most vulnerable part of me

had closed off, clenched up, contracted.

The idea that I could be reunited with these beings I'd

conceived, that we could love each other, that together we

could form a kind of whole, was so much more than I could

have ever dared to hope or believe—and yet, to me, belief in

Christ consisted, in a way, of allowing the deepest desires of

my heart to be "true"; to be capable of fulfillment. I couldn't undo what I'd done. I wasn't proposing to enter into a fairy tale. But if the blind could be made to see, if a paralytic could get up off his mat and walk, if a drunk could get sober, then maybe, unbelievable as the prospect seemed, this wound could at last begin to be healed.

"Begin," I soon learned, was the operative word. I was supposed to try to remember the abortions. I, who remember in almost comically vivid detail sights, sounds, and conversations from decades ago, remembered almost nothing: not the dates, not the faces of the doctors, not what I wore, thought about, ate, felt. I remembered bleakness, coldness, riding home on the subway in Boston alone.

I was to try to undergo the stages of grieving: denial, anger, depression, acceptance. I had to identify and be willing to let go of resentments to which I'd been holding on for decades. If I wanted freedom from bondage, I had to fully release from bondage everyone else I felt had ever done me wrong, including my family, the abortion doctors, the men I'd loved who hadn't quite loved me back (understatement!) the way I might have hoped. I had to look at my tendency toward self-justification, my perfectionism, my profound fear of abandonment which—surprise—went back to my mother.

Over the next several months, I saw the (sainted) Christine (who "charged" on a donation-only basis, by the way) almost every week. I prayed with and for the children. I spoke to them. I made my way through two thick workbooks. I wrote pages and pages—of stream-of-consciousness journal entries, of inventory.

During this process, one of my brothers sent me a photo he'd unearthed from the family archives, then thoughtfully had blown up and framed. I'd always joked about how I'd (grandiosely) taken it upon myself from a very young age to "save" my family, but this picture—of me as a kid; one I'd never seen before—shocked me into realizing that I'd come by my illusions honestly. I was standing, alone, on the front stoop of the Rhode Island farmhouse in which my mother had been raised, and I saw, as I'd never seen as a child, that the house was badly, shamefully, in need of repair: dilapidated stoop, derelict shingles, unkempt lawn. A wooden awning sagged over the doorway, behind a half-drawn curtain peeked the ghostly face of my notoriously hermit-like grandmother, and there—as the arrow loaded with eons of unworked-through baggage was launched—I stood: just shy of my sixth birthday.

Already, little feet firmly planted, hands thrust in coat pockets, I'd worn a winning, chin-up, smile. Already, emotional neglect the firm backdrop, my pose had said: *Don't worry, I'll be the glue that holds things together! We'll be okay—won't we? If I make you laugh, will you love me?...*Already, I'd been a "survivor"—as everyone in my family had been—but what generations of silent, bone-deep sorrow had I inherited? What kind of mothering could my poor mother have given me? So much pain was stored in my body and nervous system. Over and over and over again, I had felt: *This has failed. This has died. This effort, longing, love, will not be returned.* Somewhere back there I had stopped breathing. I had held my breath once, in an effort to keep the pain at bay, and I had never quite breathed freely again.

I was encouraged to put names, faces, personality characteristics to the children I'd conceived. Like my friend who'd "known" his aborted child had been male, I instantly

knew my first two had been girls and the youngest a boy.

Here, I was unabashedly influenced by *Whistle Down the

Wind*, the 1959 novel by Mary Hayley Bell in which three

children from an English village find an injured, chain-smoking,

cryptic, escaped criminal in the barn and think he's Jesus.

Which in a sense he is, as we're all Jesus: some—often

convicted criminals—more than others. The kids sneak him

food and cigarettes, protect him from the grownups, stick with

him when the cops come with the bullhorns and baying dogs

and guns. They wonder about things. They know not to go to

their parents for help. They are realistic, they know about pain,

and they also have tender hearts. Their names are Brat (short

for Brambling), Swallow, and Poor Baby.

I was supposed to make a collage. *You're joking*, was

my first thought. I'm fifty-seven years old and I'm going to cut

pictures out of *Cosmo*? I'm in existential crisis here and I'm

going to do crafts? Typically, as soon as I started I became

obsessively absorbed and spent hours poring through old

copies of *The New Yorker*, *Harper's*, *Gourmet*, *Wired*, and

Science, then gluing my gleanings to a cardboard triptych that, like Dante's *The Divine Comedy*, consisted of Hell, Purgatory, and Paradise.

Hell featured fire, knives, a loan-shark storefront, and a bottle of Gilbey's gin. Purgatory boasted a colossal waterfall (cleverly evocative of baptism), a picture of a burning bush from a Byzantine fresco, and color-stained photos of the DNA of mouse ears (for the miracle of creation!). Paradise sported a Renaissance Madonna and Child from a 1984 *Gourmet* article on Tuscan food, a girl in a leopard-skin coat jumping rope, and a William Eggleston photo: "Motel, Wildwood, New Jersey" (I pictured the four of us leaning mournfully out of separate windows—*because they'd be loners, too!*—over the eerily spot-lit swimming pool).

The crowning glory was a big blue-green sky full of clouds that were part light, part dark, with way at the top, three tiny baby heads pasted on.

Abortion leaves behind no photos, no physical objects to touch or look at or smell, no memories of flesh, nails, hair. A collage was a poor, and if you like pathetic facsimile, and it was also the closest I was ever going to come to an incarnation.

The culminating event of treatment, I'd known from the start, was to be a three-day retreat with twenty or so other women. "You're going to love this," Christine had been telling me for months. "What happens over these weekends is unbelievable."

My silent response to *You're going to love this* is invariably, *No, I'm not.* And though I was way willing to put my best foot forward, sure enough, I arrived the Friday night in question at what turned out to be a tidy, middle-America convent: not at all the medieval, shadow-shrouded abbey I would have preferred. Amy Grant tunes, not Gregorian chant, wafted down the hall. Dinner consisted of creamed chicken, canned peas, and a stupendous array of salt-, fat-, and sugar-laden snacks. I was touched to the core by the generosity of Christine and the other volunteers, but I had to sneak off by myself, wander the grounds, and avail myself of a prickly pear with salmon-gold blooms, a ruby-throated hummingbird and, over by the Dumpster, the sweet, sweet smell of orange-tree flowers mixed with garbage before I even began to feel at home.

I would just as soon have been left alone to kvetch, snack, and swap tales with my comrades, but in spite of their almost insane goodwill, the people in charge had a grueling program on tap which I learned in that night's opening session would include many group prayers, many songs I would probably not have selected myself, and a series of role-playing exercises called "Living Scripture." Plunging forthwith into the latter, we heard the parable of the adulterous woman ("Let him who is without sin cast the first stone"), after which we each rose from our seats, selected a rock from the collection that had been placed in the middle of the room, and pledged to carry it around for the weekend (including to the bathroom and our beds) as a symbol of the psychic burden we had been carrying for so long. At some later point, presumably Saturday night or Sunday, we would choose the right moment and put the rock down.

Under other circumstances I might have quailed, but If I had learned nothing in my life, I had learned "Take what you like and leave the rest." I would never have gotten sober or become a Catholic if I had not learned that reality operates on a level we can't see; that the things of this world point to a higher world. This was far from the hokiest scene I'd ever experienced, not by a long shot, and it would have been impossible not to stand in admiration and awe of the real sacrifices many people were making in order to make the weekend possible. One young girl stayed up all night praying the Rosary before the Blessed Sacrament. A lady from the Antelope Valley had made individual prayer cards for each of us. One set of volunteers consisted of a woman, her husband, and the woman's parents who had taken her to the abortion clinic when she was a teenager, all four of whom were now devoting a good part of their lives to retreats like these.

Still, by Saturday morning's third "Living Scripture" exercise I'd started to wonder, *When are we going to get to "process," or pray, or write madly in our journals?* I'm all about silence and solitude and, failing that, I'm all about story. Happily, that afternoon we were finally invited to break into small groups and "share." I am a big, *big* fan of the shared story. There is some huge transformative power in telling what it was like, what happened, and what it's like now—in your own words, at your own pace, not for the purpose of getting critiqued or commented upon or challenged, but simply in order to say: *I am here. I signify.* Also, people tend to be amazingly articulate, sincere, insightful, moving, and with luck, funny when they tell their stories—especially if events are involved of which they are not all that proud.

I found the room to which my group had been assigned, nabbed a Frisbee-sized chocolate-chip cookie from the snack table, and settled in. The range of ages, demographics, and experiences was wide. Mai, a Vietnamese woman who worked as a bank teller, had aborted after a fling with a gang banger. Narida, an airline executive, had been born in Mumbai, lived all over the world, and undergone five abortions, the last of which, coupled with the dastardly behavior of the guy in question, had prompted a major examination of conscience. An elderly gal limped in late muttering in an East European accent, "God almighty! Have they changed the schedule again? They change without telling us, no, go ahead without me. My life has been hell, HELL!"

with a small forbearing smile. This was Karel, 84, who it turned

out had survived the Nazi occupation of Czechoslovakia, had

been deported along with her abusive husband to Bolivia, had

suffered two abortions while awaiting asylum to the U.S., and

had mourned the losses every day for the intervening forty-

odd years.

I'd told my own story, or bits and pieces of it, before: in

my essays and books, in the Sacrament of Reconciliation, to

Christine. But to tell it in front of these women who understood

as no-one else could was an experience of a different order: a

different kind of vulnerability, a different kind of acceptance, a

different kind of seeing that, like them, I was a fallible human

being who had made three very wrong choices and who had

also suffered for them; had perhaps suffered long enough. I

didn't tell anything new. I didn't feel any dramatic turning-of-

the-corner release. But I did realize as I spoke that abortion is

in a way a kind of suicide. You're killing a part of yourself.

You're saying *I'm not worthy to perpetuate my place on earth,*

my spirit and soul.

A guy, a young, muscle-bound pipe fitter, was in our group well. Three years ago he and his girlfriend (who was telling her own story in a separate small group) had agreed to abort the child they'd conceived. He'd driven her to the clinic that morning, and from that day forward, had been devastated. Watching him fidgeting, wringing his hands, groping for the words to describe feelings for which no words exist, I thought: *Now that is a man. Only a man could acknowledge such anguish. Only a man could acknowledge the magnitude of his actions.* When we'd re-convened after with the other retreatants, his girlfriend was the first to speak. Watching her stare down at the floor and say, "I just want him to *love* me again," I thought: *How fragile we are, we humans. How much damage we can do.*

Lying in bed that night, unable to sleep, I reflected that the last twenty-plus years had been a kind of pruning, a purgation. I had committed the worst possible sin—the widest imaginable "missing of the mark"—and maybe I had also had to undergo the worst possible emotional pain in order to begin to heal. Although perhaps no wound that deep ever exactly heals. A wound is accepted and incorporated, just as Christ's wounds were incorporated—not removed, not erased, but incorporated—after the Resurrection. I'd undergone a purgation, and in the purgation all of reality had been accepted and incorporated, and in the incorporation, something new had been made, or was being made, of me. I was both the person who had aborted my children and the lover of Christ; both deeply selfish and deeply giving, both the Virgin Mary and Mary Magdalene—and something more besides. I would continue to stumble, to be broken and weak, to fail. But I could also live out the rest of my life in a way befitting the mother my children deserved; the mother I would liked to have been but had not been able to be; the mother who, from a supernatural standpoint, I actually was.

Sunday's schedule featured a gabfest breakfast, followed by Mass, followed by final instructions for the pièce de résistance "memorial" during which we were to mount the altar, one by one, and pay homage to our unborn child(ren): an event I, for one was heartily dreading (not least of all because I was afraid of bursting into hyperventilating tears). To prepare, I took one last walk around the grounds: marveling at the flowers, giving thanks for the sun, gathering myself. Back in my room, I wrested my haystack hair into place and donned my one skirt. I knelt on the floor by my bed and prayed: for my kids, for the other women, for all the women around the world that day who were going to have an abortion.

I arrived to find the chapel decked with fake flowers. Enough Kleenex had been laid in to stock an ER. We'd been urged to write a letter to her/him/ them, and read it out loud, but here I'd balked. For one thing, a letter is between you and the person to whom you write it, so why would I let anyone else in on it? More to the point, my kids would have been in their twenties by now. I didn't think of them as babies, actually. I thought of them as adults with their own joys, problems, likes, dislikes, and prodigious baggage that any child of mine—especially one I'd aborted—would be likely to have.

So I wormed nervously into a pew, tried to look invisible, and listened to the several others who went first; grateful, after all, for the Kleenex. The letters were affecting enough in their own right, and the family members and friends we'd been encouraged to invite, and who'd come, made for more pathos. Karel, the elderly woman from Czechoslovakia, had only recently told her 55-year-old daughter of her long-ago abortions; instead of disowning her, as Karel had feared, the daughter had shown up for the service and could not have been more beautiful, gracious, or kind. Mai, the Vietnamese woman who'd conceived with a gang banger, was sitting with her husband and four-year-old son. The pipe fitter guy who'd brought his girlfriend to the clinic was front and center with his parents. My own buddy Yvonne had made the trek across town and was lending moral support from a few pews back.

Right up till the last minute, I wasn't sure what I'd say.

I had no letter.

I had only my heart that had been yearning toward these three children since the day they were conceived. I had only my conscience, which knew what I had done was wrong. When my turn came, I walked up front, mounted the stairs to the altar, took my place behind the lectern, and said, "This is how I picture my kids":

Fern, my oldest, looks out for the others. Organized, feisty, a scientist of some kind maybe. Deeply smart, sensitive, does not show much but feels keenly. She loves me, but is also, understandably, slightly pissed/hurt and suspicious still as well.

My middle child, a girl, Swallow. Gentle, funny, flies up to her nest in the eaves and ponders. She has books stashed up there and a small cache of snacks and refreshes herself, prays, then gathers herself and goes out and is cheerful and has a wry joke and shores people up in a way that doesn't draw attention to itself so that people never know how much she gives away and how deep the cost.

My youngest, a boy, Warren. Lives outside society. In trouble somehow. Worries about his father and me.

I'd meant to read a Wislawa Szymborska poem—"Return Baggage"—but instead I looked out over the faces of those women and men with whom I'd been in the trenches all weekend and blurted, "I should have laid down my lives for my children, and instead they laid theirs down for me."

I hadn't meant to say it—I'd never even thought such a thing before—and yet it was true. They had died in a sense so I could live. Without the anguish I had felt on their behalf, I might never have been driven to get sober. Without the keening of my heart, I might never have felt spurred to move to L.A., to find my way to Christ, to start writing. They had sent me off, and accompanied me, on a long, long journey. They had suffered annihilation without a word of reproach and now at long last they had risen up, become visible, appeared, and—in a manner that couldn't have happened otherwise—I had, too.

Did the children have to die so that I could be born? No, that couldn't be. But maybe, as St. Thomas Aquinas surmised, "God allows evils to happen in order to bring a greater good therefrom."

And then I stepped down to a receiving line of hugs, a white rose, and a certificate with the kids' names on it saying they were in heaven.

"Hang tough, guys," I told them in the ladies' room after. "Just one more round of 'refreshments,' and then we can bolt."

Nibbling cake topped with lard-laced frosting and exchanging e-mail addresses later, I reflected that hardly a moment of the weekend had jibed with my aesthetic and spiritual "sensibility," but what ever, really, does, unless your own apartment?—which, let's face it, you can't stay in forever. "The man of solitude is happy, but he never has a good time," Thomas Merton had observed, and though I hadn't had a "good time," reluctant to leave this charmed circle, I ended up being among the last to leave. I was incoherently grateful to Christine and the other immensely kind, generous, self-emptying people who had helped put on the retreat. I felt profoundly bonded to the other women and men who had shared themselves, their stories, their pain. And cornball as the "Carrying the Stone" exercise had been, somehow, sometime during that weekend, a gigantic chunk of the burden I'd been carrying for all those years had lifted.

St. Paul had mercilessly persecuted the early Christians. St. Augustine had been a slave to lust before he surrendered his entire self to God. Dorothy Day, called by some the most influential Catholic laywoman of the twentieth century, had had an abortion before she'd converted. If they'd been forgiven, surely I had been, too. If they'd moved on, surely that was my obligation as well. But first, I had needed to forgive myself. I had needed to be reminded that my fear that there would not be enough—money, support, love—had been learned, not willfully, spitefully cultivated. And maybe most of all, I had needed to sit in a circle with other women who had mourned in silence, who had secretly keened, who had had no-one with whom to talk: no support, no exit, no voice.

Had not the whole weekend, in fact, been the clearest possible example of Christ in action; of people doing for us— loving us, supporting us, sacrificing for us, guiding us—what we cannot do for ourselves? To love Christ is to give to another what we lack, but long to have ourselves—and in the giving, the lack is somehow fulfilled. That is a realization, an orientation of heart, an approach to life that cannot be legislated. That is an orientation of heart that is granted as a gift—almost always, it seems, after great, great pain. And the sign of an authentic gift, and an authentic receipt, is that you want nothing more from that point forward than to give the gift to others.

Packing up my car, I thought of all the hokey things folks tend to mention—first snowfalls, idyllic summer afternoons—in their odes to the kids they didn't have the time or money or hope for. *Not me*, I thought, gazing across the acres of strangely endearing dreck, the exhaust-shrouded palm trees, the stray star beginning to burn through the smog. *I'm sorry they missed this*: the whole weird, inarticulable, excruciatingly painful, exultantly joyful, through-a-glass-darkly experience that for all the failure, disappointment, bewilderment, loneliness, and loss, I myself wouldn't have missed for anything in the world.

I was sorry they'd missed all that but, headed home, I also couldn't imagine my life any other way than the way it was. I'm not sure I would have had it any other way than the way it was. Even now, I didn't particularly regret not having children. I regretted the violence, the blindness. I regretted that those particular children hadn't been born. But I also

believed I would meet them some day. I had mourned them

for twenty years and now I could look them in the eye and tell

them I was sorry. I had established a relationship with them

and the relationship would be ongoing. You don't feel as badly

as I did, for as long as I had, except out of love. They had

shown me that I did have a capacity for love. They had

reminded me that for all my wrong turns, I had always

hungered to draw the world to my breast. They had connected

me to the fierce, creatively self-giving life force of all mothers

and all women. They had taught me that my task now would

be to lay down my life for other people's children. They had

given me a humble and contrite heart. They had rendered me,

finally, worthy of my suffering.

The 10 freeway can be an extreme sport, especially

after dark: the taillights red in the inky night, the silhouette of

County Hospital, the way I'd lived in L.A so long I knew to

merge left before the 710 came up, to stay in the right

lane after the hair-pin curve and zip by the backed-up traffic

waiting to get onto the 5, in the thick of downtown to move a couple of lanes left again as the "Exit Only" lane for the 110 loomed.

Semis barreled by. A lane-cutting motorcyclist nearly nicked my fender. I wondered, as I often do while driving the freeways, if I'd emerge intact, then swerved onto the Vermont/Hoover bypass, cut across four lanes of traffic, and exited at Normandie: one more time, almost home; one more time, safe.

The air smelled of oleanders and frying meat. Streetlamps cast haloes of sallow light on the folks ranged up and down the block like characters in a modern-day Passion Play. A panhandler held a sign saying, "Why Lie? I Need a Beer." A guy in a wheelchair hawked pineapples from the back of a battered truck. A tattooed teenaged girl, heavily pregnant, peered anxiously up the street for the bus.

My brothers and sisters…My daughters! My sons! *O felix culpa quae talem et tantum meruit habere redemptorem*," we sing each year at the Easter Vigil—the night Christ was resurrected: "O happy fault that merited such and so great a Redeemer."

Heather King is the author of three memoirs: *Parched* (New American Library 2005); *Redeemed: Stumbling Toward God, Marginal Sanity, and the Peace That Passes All Understanding* (Viking 2008); and *Shirt of Flame: A Year with St. Thérèse of Lisieux* (Paraclete 2011). She is a sober alcoholic, an ex-lawyer, a Catholic convert, and a full-time writer. She lives in Los Angeles and blogs at *Shirt of Flame: Musings on Los Angeles, The Writing Life, Divine Intoxication, and The Thin Line Between Passion and Pathology* (shirtofflame.blogspot.com).

For more information, visit her website at heather-king.com.

Made in the USA
Lexington, KY
19 September 2012